Author: Jae Logan
Kids That Care Books

First edition
Printed in the United States of America

www.JaeLogan.com

Kids That Care Books are books meant to show that children are capable of more than we think. Their endless love and compassion can change lives. They are capable of supporting their parents, friends, and family members in ways we cannot comprehend until we experience it.

I hope you experience that support in my books and share them with your families and friends.

Acknowledgments

This book is dedicated to the wild minds of Marla Fisher, Everett, Everett Jr. & Gabby. This idea from a friend grew and grew in my house until out exploded this book. Thank you for your love and support.

Thank you to all the dogs in this book that I know in real life, for allowing me to use your likeness. I hope you feel these images do you justice. I also hope that this enlightens human families to the lives of dogs.

To my readers, I hope that as you read this book to your dogs, you add in a sprinkle of words that elicit reactions from them. Tag me in pictures and reels @JaeLoganAuthor on IG.

Want to purchase an autographed copy?
Contact me through my website or check out my calendar of events at:

www.jaelogan.com

or

www.kidsthatcarebooks.com

Hello! My name is Sandy. I am a good dog! Sometimes my name is Sandy NO! That is when I am not being a good girl. Here are some of my favorite things and friends.

Hank and Maxine! Good job on the sitting!! Do you sit? I love to sit! When I sit, I get a treat! Sit, while you learn about my favorite things. Maybe the person reading this will give you a treat!

Bailey found the treats! Good girl! I love treats.
Bailey, can you give me some treats? Or save me
some treats? Treats are the best!

I love going to the park! Do you love going to the park? Did you know that park rhymes with bark? Park. Bark!

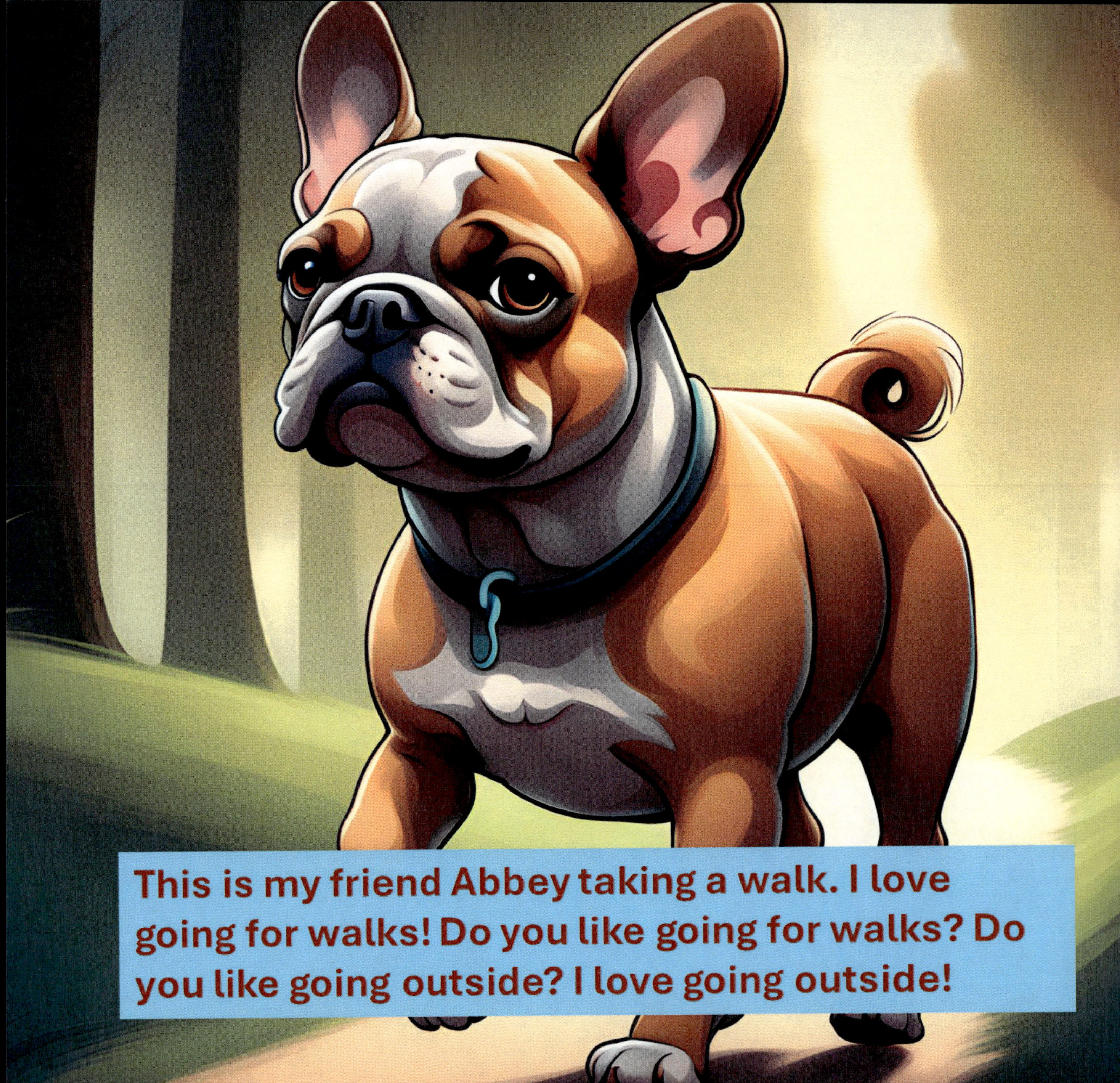
This is my friend Abbey taking a walk. I love going for walks! Do you like going for walks? Do you like going outside? I love going outside!

SQUIRREL!!

Squirrels make us.. WOOF! WOOF! WOOF! WOOF! WOOF! ARF! ARF! GRRRRR! GRRR! WOOF! This is Hudson on squirrel watch.

This is my friend Charles. He loves to chase rabbits! Do you like to chase rabbits? Do you run a lot? Running outside is my favorite!

Do you like to play catch or fetch? My friend Ringo plays fetch! I like catch. Sometimes I play fetch, but catch is more fun!

This is Simba. Simba knows tricks. Here he is doing “shake”. Do you know how to shake? Shake! I shake with my family so that they will give me treats.

High five is another trick that a dog can use for treats. Misty is going all out and lifting both paws up to touch her human parent's hands. They LOVE that! Misty gets extra treats for that!

When Mocha jumps they throw the treats at her, so she can catch them. It is a fun game that ends up in extra treats! Can you jump? Jump!!

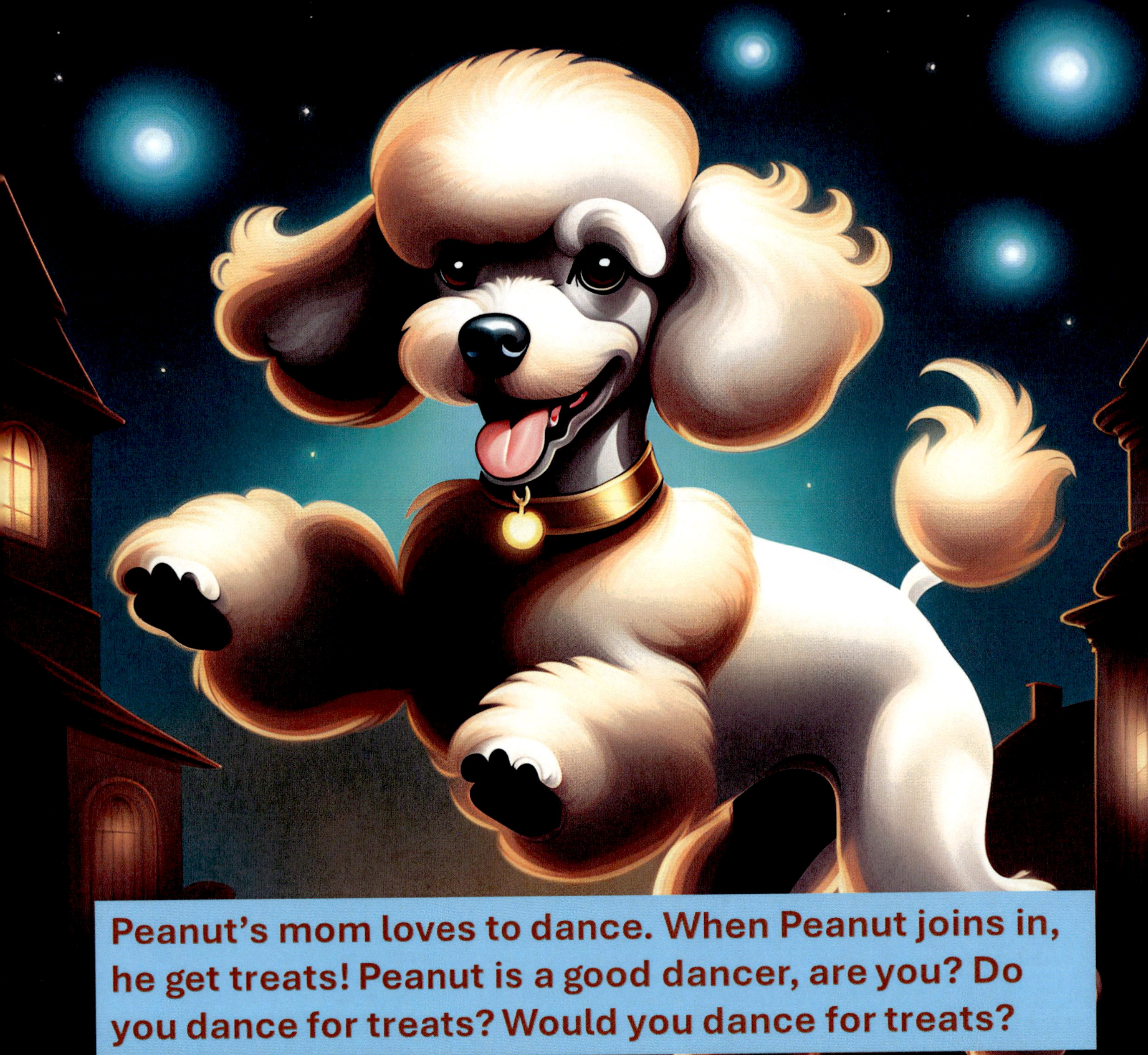

Peanut's mom loves to dance. When Peanut joins in, he get treats! Peanut is a good dancer, are you? Do you dance for treats? Would you dance for treats?

Stella keeps guard by the door. There are always people at the door in her house. She has to protect her family from intruders!! Grrrrrrr!!! Who's at the door? Get the door!!

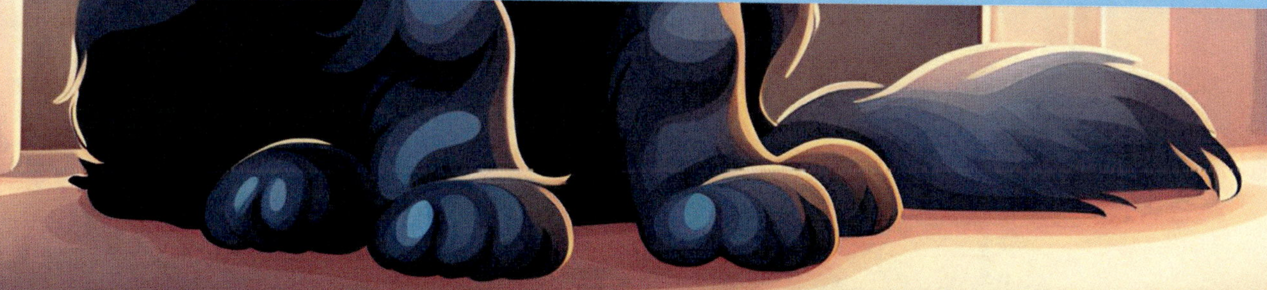

GRRRRRR the delivery people always make me angry! They smell like the whole neighborhood! I don't trust them. WOOOF!! WOOF!! GRRRRRR!!!!

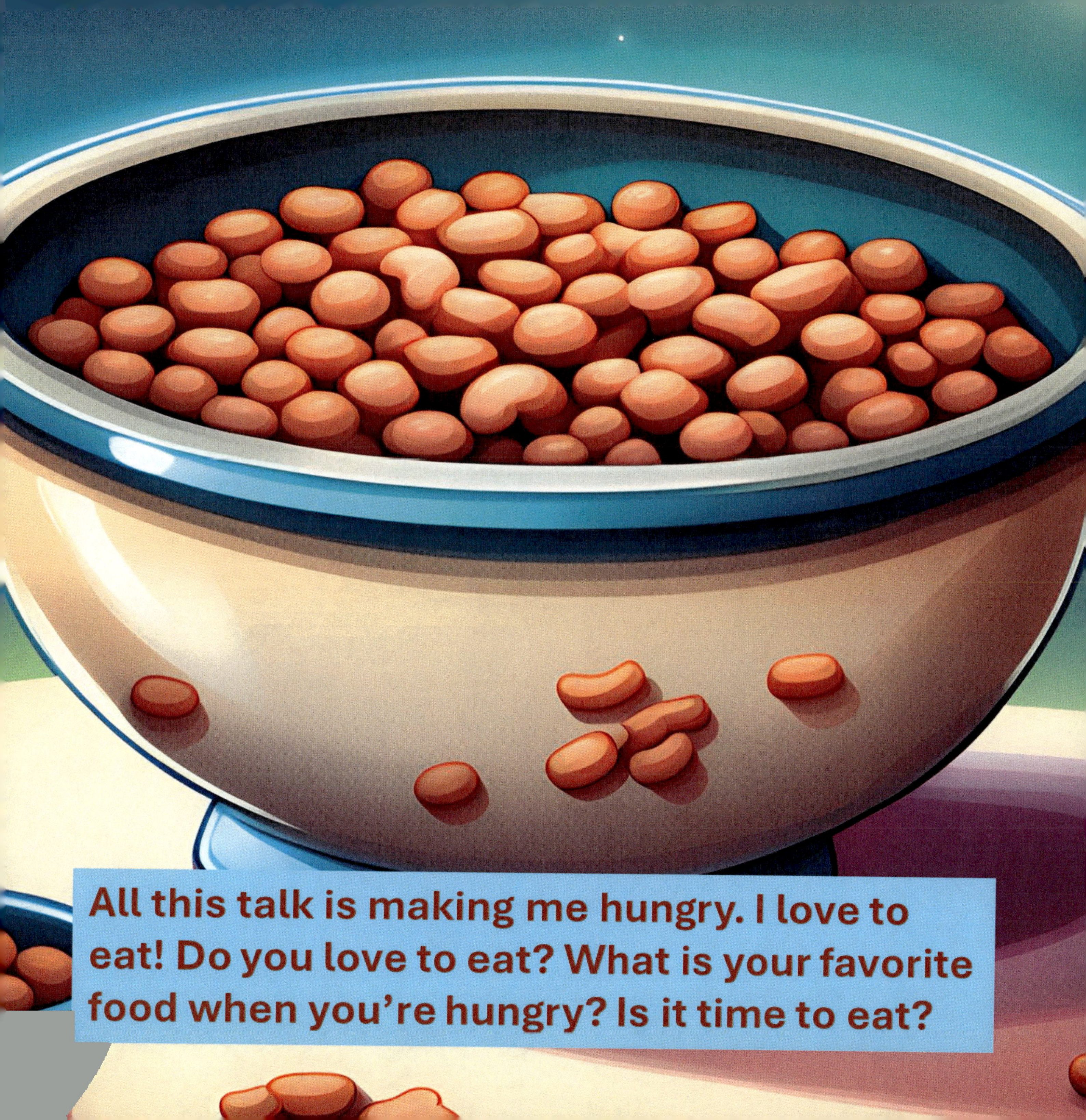
All this talk is making me hungry. I love to eat! Do you love to eat? What is your favorite food when you're hungry? Is it time to eat?

Do you love kisses, hugs, and cuddles? I love kisses!! Do you give kisses? Jasper gives the best kisses according to his human Mom!

My friend Oliver taught me how to lay down. He does it all the time! And guess what? He gets treats for doing it! A snack and a nap? That's wonderful!

This is my friend Cindy. She is waiting patiently for a treat. Do you wait patiently for treats? Is it treat time?

I hope you learned a lot today. I am tired now! I am going to bed! Night! Night!

This is the 3rd book by Kids That Care Books. Here is a summary of the first two books. All books are currently available on Amazon.

Mommy Doesn't Look Sick

Gabby and Evy love to have fun with their parents, they do all sorts of activities. One day Mommy is diagnosed with an invisible illness, and it is hard for the children to understand that she is sick because she does not look sick. The children learn that while mom may be in the hospital sick it does not mean that she loves them any less. Together they learn to deal with Mom's new illness and still enjoy the fun and games they did before she was in the hospital.

Holiday Cookies

Join Kevin on an epic cookie adventure! As he delivers cookies, he discovers so many cool holidays like Hanukkah, Diwali, and even Kwanzaa. From shiny gold shopping to super-fast fire poles, there's never a dull moment. Dive into a world where every day is a party, and every tradition is a new treat to learn about. Get ready for a journey filled with yummy cookies, bright lights, and amazing stories from friends.

With Kevin, every holiday is a delicious discovery!

About the Author

I am a Puerto Rican woman from NYC. I was raised by amazing parents that were the perfect combination of supportive and tough on me. I appreciate it, I didn't when I was younger, but I do now that I have kids.
Kids are tough, but they are also so much fun.

I love my kids more than I can ever find the words to explain. They are amazing to talk to and raise. They can be a headache at times, but they are fun human beings that truly care about others.

It is also with them in mind that I launched Kids That Care Books.

Keep an eye out for the Spanish translations of my books.

Made in the USA
Middletown, DE
28 July 2024